Angela Gray's
Cookery School
Summer Recipes

Photographs Huw Jones

Summer Recipes
Angela Gray's Cookery School
Published in Great Britain in 2017 by
Graffeg Limited

Written by Angela Gray copyright © 2017.
Food photography by Huw Jones
copyright © 2017.
Food styling by André Moore.
Designed and produced by Graffeg Limited
copyright © 2017

Graffeg Limited, 24 Stradey Park Business
Centre, Mwrwg Road, Llangennech,
Llanelli, Carmarthenshire SA14 8YP Wales
UK Tel 01554 824000 www.graffeg.com

ISBN 9781912050000

1 2 3 4 5 6 7 8 9

Photo credits

Pages 6-147 and end papers © Huw Jones

Pages 147, 148, 150-151, 152, 153, 154, 156
© A L S Photography
www.alsphotography.co.uk

Angela Gray's

Cookery School

Summer Recipes

Photographs Huw Jones

GRAFFEG

Contents

Desserts

Introduction

Welcome to my summer kitchen, where I draw inspiration from the delicious seasonal larder to recreate a collection of recipes that I have shared with friends, family and guests over the years.

There's nothing quite like a clear blue sky and the feeling of warmth from the sun on your skin. For me it's an instant tonic, I can close my eyes and be instantly transported to any number of sunny places that hold special memories. From picking soft summer fruits in our farm garden growing up in Wales, to working in the South of France where I found an abundance of sun-ripened ingredients that would forever change the way I cook.

Despite the very changeable and unpredictable summer climate in Britain, I do remember long, hot summer days growing up.

When I was very young and lived in Porthcawl, the beach always beckoned and my mum and I would often have a simple picnic of cheese and tomato sandwiches and a slice of homemade cake or fruit tart to enjoy as the sun beamed low in the sky.

Picnics were commonplace growing up, from a special family day out at The Royal Welsh Show, to a car picnic on a long journey. I have always loved dining al fresco, the outdoors seems to sharpen the appetite and senses, so the enjoyment of eating is heightened. A beautiful view always helps too!

There were many lovely views to come when I embarked on my career as a chef and travelled to work abroad. I remember one job very clearly when I arrived in Nice to work privately for Andrew Lloyd-Weber in St-Jean-Cap-Ferrat. The scenery, the quality of light and intensity of the sun just captivated me. It was like staring at a Dufy painting and I knew in an instant that this would be an adventure.

My first evening in St. Jean was wonderful. Having been introduced to my new boss, I was invited out for supper by Bill (the chauffeur) who had booked a table at a local eatery overlooking the bay. I remember the scent of flowers and herbs that permeated the air during the early evening as we walked along to the restaurant and the amazing aromas that greeted us as we arrived.

We ate simply – anchoiade, tapenade and aioli with raw summer vegetables and little toasts, then locally caught John Dory simply cooked with olive oil and Herbs de Provence, baked sun-ripe tomatoes and a green salad, followed by baked peaches with a raspberry sauce. How could simplicity taste so utterly delicious? I was smitten, I couldn't wait to start cooking and was eager to find the best places to buy the ingredients for the menus that I would prepare.

The next day, Bill took me Beaulieu-sur-Mer and that was it, I had found my utopia. I would come here almost daily, early in the morning to experience the vibe and an abundance of possibilities. Everything was local – fish, crustaceans, meat, poultry, cheese, vegetables, fruits, herbs and flowers and so much more – I was having the time of my life shopping! I would create my menus as I walked around and couldn't wait to get back to the kitchen to cook – I felt so alive – I had found my culinary mojo!

So much of this passion is re-lived

through the recipes in this book. I have used a palette of robust flavours, beautiful colours and varied textures. Herbs, olives, garlic, citrus, anchovies, chilli, wines and liqueurs are all used in various ways to bring a distinctive character to a dish. The simple recipe for pesto demonstrates this beautifully – vivid colour, powerful flavour and a nutty texture. This simple paste of five ingredients defines that wonderful fusion between the South of France and Italy and you can create a little bit of this in your own kitchen!

Memories of cooking in St. Jean are still so vivid. I can see the large dining table on the terrace overlooking the Mediterranean, the smell of fresh cut flowers and herbs in bowls on the table, a little piano music echoing through the house, the aromas of cooking building in the kitchen and me feeling totally inspired and enjoying every moment.

My travels to France, Italy, Spain, Greece, Canada (especially for barbecuing!) and indeed being home here in Wales have all helped to shape my recipes, and although we are not always blessed with a good sunny climate here in Britain, we still have a superb larder of seasonal ingredients to hand. They may be subtler in flavour than those in hotter climates, but we can still create great dishes from them.

As summer approaches, I will be planning our schedule for the Cookery School, as well as a few social gatherings with friends and family. There will still be bowls of flowers and herbs on the table, a little background music and the aromas of cooking oozing from the kitchen. We may not have a view of the sea from our garden terrace (decking!), but we will have great food, good wine and that's enough for me.

Angela Gray

Pissaladiére

A simple, yet utterly delicious traditional bread from the South of France. I discovered it on a day off in St. Jean and purchased a hearty slice for my picnic at the beach. It was so good – sun, sea, stunning views and my pissaladiére!

Ingredients

For the base

400g bread flour

7g fast-action yeast

1 level teaspoon fine sea salt

100ml warm water

1 free-range egg

50g butter, melted

50ml olive oil

For the topping

1kg onions, peeled and thinly sliced

6 tablespoons olive oil

6 tablespoons of water

6 stems thyme, leaves only

Sea salt and black pepper

12 anchovy fillets

16 good black olives

Serves 6-8

What you do

1 First, make the base for the pissaladiére – place the flour in a large mixing bowl together with the yeast, use your hand to stir in the salt and combine all the dry ingredients. Make a well in the centre and break in the egg, pour in the warm water, the melted butter and olive oil. Mix the wet ingredients together briefly and then incorporate with the dry ingredients. Push together to form a smooth, soft dough. Pop into a lightly oiled bowl, cover with a tea towel and leave in a warm place to double in size, this could take up to 2 hours.

2 Meanwhile cook the onions – heat the olive oil over a medium heat, add the onions and stir through. Add the water, place a lid over the pan and sweat the onions, stirring occasionally until really soft. Remove the lid, add the thyme leaves, 1 flat teaspoon of sea salt and ¼ teaspoon of fresh, ground black pepper, stir through. Continue cooking the onions until any liquid has evaporated – be careful not to brown them.

③ Preheat the oven to 180°C/Fan 160°C/Gas 4.

④ Roll out the dough into a 28cm circle or make a rectangle, depending on the shape of your baking sheet. Lift on to an oiled baking-tray, turn up the edges to create a border the depth of your little finger. Spread the onion mixture over the dough in a thin, even layer. To finish, criss-cross the anchovies and dot all over with the olives, pushing them into the dough slightly.

⑤ Bake for 35 to 40 minutes until crisp at the edges and lightly golden on top.

The secret to getting the flavour right on this is by cooking the onions low and slow to get that sweetness which is so dynamic with the saltiness of the anchovies and olives.

Coca Bread

Coca Bread is a Catalonian flatbread. I call this my welcome bread; it sets the scene for a relaxed and enjoyable feast with friends. It's also a real favourite at the Cookery School.

Ingredients

Dough

450g strong bread flour
5g sea salt
7g fast action yeast
1 flat teaspoon caster sugar
60g of extra virgin olive oil
300ml warm water

Topping

2 medium onions
2 sweet peppers
1 aubergine
8 cherry tomatoes
12 black grapes
100g Manchego cheese

Emulsion

4 tablespoons olive oil
1 tablespoon lemon juice
1 level teaspoon sweet smoked red paprika
1 fat garlic clove, grated
1 level teaspoon sea salt
1 rounded teaspoon chopped herbs
e.g. sage, rosemary or oregano

Serves 6-8

What you do

① First, prepare the dough – in a large mixing bowl, mix together the flour, salt, fast action yeast and sugar. Make a well in the centre and pour in the olive oil and ½ of the warm water. Mix briefly with open fingers, then slowly add enough of the remaining water to form a smooth elastic dough.
Note: You may need a little more water depending on the flour.

② Pour a tablespoon of olive oil on to your work surface and spread it out with your hands to form a no-stick area. Pick up the dough and throw it forward on to the oiled surface still holding on to one end so it elongates out on the surface. Claw the dough backwards into a ball. Repeat this about 20 times until the dough firms up. Place in a lightly oiled bowl, cover and leave at room temperature until doubled in size.

③ Meanwhile, prepare the vegetables. Line 2 baking sheets

with foil or parchment paper. Peel and cut each of the onions into 8 wedges, place on the baking sheet and drizzle with a little olive oil. Roast the onions for about 30 minutes, until soft at 200°C/Fan 180°C/Gas 6.

④ Next, prepare the peppers, cut them in half, remove the stork, membrane and seeds, cut in half again. Add to the tray with the onions, drizzle with a little oil, return to the oven, the peppers need about 25 minutes. Now the aubergine, cut in half lengthways and then into medium sized half moons. Place on the second sheet, drizzle with olive oil and roast. Once the aubergines are in the oven, the vegetables should take about 20 minutes to finish cooking. **Note:** they need to be soft, not too brown. Cut the cherry tomatoes and grapes in half and cut the cheese into thin wedges.

⑤ Once the dough is ready, tip out on to the surface. Pick up the edges and bring them to the centre creating a fold, pushing down at the centre, to create a large upside-down mushroom shape. Turn the dough over so the smooth side is facing you and use your palms to flatten the dough, pressing out any air bubbles.

⑥ Place on an oiled baking sheet and, starting from the centre, knuckle the dough outwards to fit the tin. Stretch out the corners then release back into the tin to get them to fit nicely.

⑦ Prepare the emulsion by mixing everything together. Pour over the dough and spread with a brush. Arrange the vegetables, fruit and cheese in panels along the dough, so that when you cut a strip across the bread, you get a little of everything. Finish with the olives and a little drizzle of olive oil.

⑧ Bake at 220°C/Fan 200°C/Gas 7 until crisp and golden. This should take around 25 minutes. If the dough is a little soft in the middle, reduce the temperature to 180°C/Fan 160°C/Gas 5 and cover with foil and cook for a further 10 minutes.

Slow-Roasted Tomatoes with Garlic and Herbs de Provence

Ingredients

16 medium tomatoes
4 tablespoons olive oil
1 flat dessertspoon sea salt
½ teaspoon fresh ground black pepper
1 rounded teaspoon caster sugar
2 fat garlic cloves, each cut into 8 slivers

To finish

2 teaspoons Herbs de Provence

Serves 6-8

What you do

1 Line a large baking sheet with parchment paper and sprinkle with a little sea salt and black pepper. Drizzle with a tablespoon of the olive oil. Cut the tomatoes in half around the middle, place on the parchment paper and brush with the remaining olive oil.

2 Mix together the sea salt, ground pepper, and caster sugar and then sprinkle over each of the tomato halves.

3 Stud each tomato with a slither of garlic and roast sliced side up in a preheated oven 160°C/Fan 140°C/Gas 3 for about 2 hours. The tomatoes should be shrivelled and slightly brown on the edges, and smell like tomato jam. Half way through the cooking time, sprinkle with the Herbs de Provence.

4 Remove from the oven and, once cooled, pop into a sterilised kilner jar and cover with olive, sunflower or rapeseed oil and seal. They will keep for a good month in the fridge. Use in salads, on bruschetta, as a base for simple pasta sauces and as an accompaniment for fish and roast meats.

These are a summer essential for me both at home and at the School. They are so deliciously versatile in salads, topping bruschetta, with pasta and pilafs, they add intense flavour to sauces and go really well with just about anything.

Pesto Genovese

I fell in love with basil when I worked in the South of France. I brought pots and pots of it for the kitchen garden where I worked and made fresh pesto with the leaves and local pine nuts. Once you have made it by hand, there's just no going back to a jar!

Ingredients

125g fresh picked basil leaves

45g pine nuts

80g good quality Parmigiano Reggiano or Grana Padano cheese

2 fat garlic cloves

12g soft sea salt flakes

100ml extra virgin olive oil

Serves 6-8

What you do

1 One way is to load all of the ingredients into a food processor and blitz together to form a loose paste. However, the real way to make pesto, and to capture the essence of the flavour and the texture, is by using a pestle and mortar.

2 Place the salt in the base of the mortar, add the basil leaves, pine nuts and garlic. Rotate the pestle to grind the ingredients down – the salt helps to do this. When this starts to happen, add in the cheese a little at a time. Now start to pour in the olive oil a little at a time until incorporated. You should have a divine textured pesto with superb flavour.

3 Keep in an airtight jar with a layer of olive oil over the top. It should keep for a good week in the fridge.

This is such a versatile sauce, it is so delicious tossed though hot pasta or drizzled on top of tomato and mozzarella bruschetta and then grilled.
I also use it as a stuffing by combining breadcrumbs to firm up the texture, this can then be packed on to fish fillets and baked, or as I have used it in the ballotine of chicken on p102.

Mezze
Picnic Jars

Marinated Olives

Ingredients

300g good quality olives

6 tablespoons olive oil

1 tablespoon sherry vinegar

3 strips of lemon peel

1 bay leaf

1 fat garlic clove, thinly sliced

1 teaspoon finely chopped soft herbs
e.g. parsley, chives, dill

What you do

1 Simply mix everything together
in a bowl, cover and refrigerate until
needed. Leave at room temperature
half an hour before serving.

2 You can pop everything into a
nice sterilised Kilner jar and keep
in the fridge. If you want to keep for
a few days, top up with olive oil so
that everything is covered.

This little mix of goodies in jars make a great
picnic indoors or al fresco. For supper, I love
serving them with a platter of the courgette
fritters and some slow-roasted tomatoes.
Add some good bread to mop up the juices
and a glass or two of good wine, sorted!

Marinated Feta

Ingredients

250g block of feta, cubed

1 fat garlic clove, thinly sliced

1 medium chilli, split

2 sprigs rosemary, lightly bashed

2 bay leaves

½ a lemon, thinly sliced

300ml olive oil

What you do

1 Simply layer everything in a jar and pour in the olive oil.

2 Make sure the cheese is covered and it will last in the fridge for up to 7 days.

3 Use the oil as a dressing or for roasting vegetables – delish!

Slow-Roasted Vegetable Antipasto

Ingredients

4 sweet peppers

1 large aubergine

2 medium red onions

12 small tomatoes, halved

2 small courgettes

Olive oil for drizzling

1 dessertspoon sea salt

½ teaspoon fresh ground black pepper

1 rounded teaspoon sugar

1 fat garlic clove, cut into slivers

1 tablespoon fresh Herbs de Provence

Good balsamic vinegar for drizzling (optional)

What you do

1 Prepare the vegetables first – cut the peppers in half, remove the stork, membrane and seeds, tap each halve to ensure all the seeds are out. Cut the aubergine in half, remove the stork and then cut each half into 8 long slices. Cut the onions in half and then each half in 6 wedges. Use a wide head vegetable peeler to slice the courgette into ribbons.

2 To cook the vegetables, place the peppers, aubergine and onion on a baking sheet lined with parchment paper. Drizzle or brush with olive oil, mix together the salt, pepper and sugar and sprinkle evenly over everything – reserve some for seasoning the tomatoes and courgettes. Roast at 190°C/Fan 170°C/Gas 5 for 30 minutes until they start to soften and turn brown at the edges.

3 Add the tomatoes to the tray, or cook on a separate tray if it's too much of a squeeze. Brush or drizzle with olive oil, stud each tomato with a sliver of garlic and sprinkle with some of the remaining seasoning.

4 Return everything to the oven, reduce the temperature to 150°C/Fan 130°C/Gas 2 and roast for about 40 minutes, the tomatoes should be slightly shrivelled and the other vegetables beautifully soft. Ten minutes before the cooking time is complete, add the courgette ribbons to the vegetables, season, brush with olive oil and return to the oven to complete the cooking, about 5 minutes.

5 Remove from the oven and cover with the herbs.

6 You can layer the vegetables in a sterilised Kilner jar and top them up with olive oil. Keep in the fridge for up to a week. When you serve them, you can drizzle a little balsamic or sherry vinegar over the top for a delicious finish.

Courgette
Fritter Platter

Ingredients

Fritters

75g grated potato
½ small onion, very thinly sliced
1 fat garlic clove, grated with a little sea salt
200g courgette, coarsely grated
½ teaspoon sea salt
1 medium free-range egg
2 sprigs mint, leaves chopped
3 sprigs parsley, leaves chopped
¼ teaspoon black pepper
25g self-raising flour

Stuffed courgette flowers

6 courgette flowers
200g ricotta or soft goat's cheese
2 tablespoons grated Parmesan
1 dessertspoon Greek yoghurt
1 free-range egg yolk
1 tablespoon chopped soft herbs e.g. basil, chives, parsley
¼ teaspoon sea salt and a pinch of black pepper

Batter

75g plain flour
30g cornflour
½ teaspoon baking powder
200ml chilled sparkling water
Sunflower or olive oil for frying

Serves 6

What you do

1 First, prepare the stuffed courgette flowers. Mix together the cheeses, Greek yoghurt, egg yolk, herbs and season with ¼ teaspoon sea salt and a pinch of black pepper. Open the flowers and spoon or pipe the mixture inside to fill each flower, leaving the ends free to close in the filling.

2 Mix together the batter and set aside whilst you make the fritters.

3 Place all the ingredients for the fritters in a bowl and mix together. You may need a little more flour depending on the moisture level in the potato and courgette. The finished mixture should be thick and creamy.

4 Heat a large/wide pan ¼ filled with sunflower/olive oil, pop a little of the fritter mixture to test the heat. When it starts to sizzle add a dessertspoon of the mixture, about 6 at a time, and cook until a medium golden colour, turn over to complete the cooking. Drain well on double-layered kitchen paper. Keep warm in the oven at 70°C/Fan 50°C/Gas ½.

5 To cook the flowers, dip each into the batter holding on to the flower tip so the filling stays intact. Allow excess batter to run off the flower, then carefully ease it into the oil. Cook 3 at a time until lightly golden, turning half way through to ensure even cooking. Drain well.

6 Plate the fritters and flowers, garnish with summer herbs and salad leaves. Serve with yogurt and herb dip or roasted pepper sauce (see page 68).

Yoghurt dip

200g Greek yoghurt, ¼ teaspoon sea salt, pinch of black pepper, 2 tablespoons mixed, chopped herbs, 1 teaspoon white wine vinegar – mix together, cover and chill until needed.

I love these, especially when I can get my hands on the flowers. These were one of Andrew Lloyd Webber's favourites and I often made them as part of a Mediterranean feast during my time in St. Jean.

Aubergine and Mozzarella Sandwiches with Tomato and Roast Pepper Sauce

Crispy sandwiches with a gooey cheese centre, so good!

Ingredients

1 large aubergine cut into 8 rounds

Olive oil

200g buffalo mozzarella cheese

16 basil leaves

Sea salt and pepper

2 medium free-range eggs + 50ml cold water

300g breadcrumbs (focaccia or panko breadcrumbs are great)

Olive oil for frying

To serve

1 quantity roast tomato and red pepper sauce (see page 68)

Serves 4 or 8 as a small starter

What you do

1 Heat a large pan, brush the aubergine slices all over with olive oil and fry in batches until golden on both sides, drain well on kitchen paper.

2 To make the sandwiches, cut the mozzarella into 4 thick slices, place one on 4 of the aubergine slices and top with 2 leaves of basil. Season with a little sprinkle of salt and pepper, top with the other slices of aubergine to create the sandwich. Squash together lightly to compact.

3 Mix together the eggs and water and dip each sandwich in the breadcrumbs, coat them all over and pat so that they stick. Shake off the excess and place on a plate ready to fry.

4 Heat a large frying pan and add enough olive oil to shallow fry the sandwiches. Fry over a medium heat so that the crumbs crisp gradually to a medium golden brown and have a delicious crisp finish.

A simple mix of rocket leaves dressed with a little lemon juice, piquant green olives and a few capers balance this dish beautifully.

Niçoise Salad

I love the way this classic salad brings together some of the best ingredients from the region of its origin. I have added in a few touches of my own, but it's still sunny Nice on a plate.

Ingredients

4 tablespoons olive oil

Salt and pepper

200g cooked new potatoes, thickly sliced

½ red onion, sliced thinly

4 x 150g fish fillets – tuna, salmon, John Dory or bass – or king prawns with the shell on

Salad

1 large cos lettuce, washed
100g cooked French green beans
A handful of slow-roasted tomatoes (see page 20)
A heaped tablespoon of olives
A teaspoon of capers
2 soft boiled free-range eggs, shelled and halved
4 anchovies in brine, halved lengthways

To finish

1 quantity vinaigrette
A small bunch of soft summer herbs, chopped e.g. parsley, chives, fennel

What you do

1 Heat 2 tablespoons of olive oil in a large frying pan, add the potato slices, sprinkle with sea salt and black pepper, fry until brown and crisp, add the onions towards the end and cook until soft – drain well on kitchen paper.

2 Wipe the pan with kitchen paper and reheat with the remaining olive oil. Add the fish fillets, season with sea salt and pepper and cook until golden on both sides. If using salmon, do most of the cooking on the skin side, approximately 6 minutes before turning, a further 4 minutes skin side up, then rest for 4 minutes. The same for the bass and John Dory, just 6 minutes on the skin side and 3 on the other side. Tuna steaks need less cooking, just 2 minutes each side. You can cook the prawns in the same way, they should be beautifully pink and slightly browned, about 3-4 minutes on each side, depending on how large the prawns are.

To assemble the salad, cut the cos lettuce into 8 wedges and place on a large serving plate arranged like a lily pad, top with fish fillets, potatoes and onions. Mix together the green beans, tomatoes, olives and capers and spoon between and over the fish.

3 Drizzle with the vinaigrette dressing and finish with the chopped herbs.

4 Finish with the halves of egg then lay the strips of anchovy over the top of the finished salad.

Vinaigrette

Place 1 small garlic clove, finely grated, 2 tablespoons white wine vinegar and 2 teaspoons Dijon mustard into a small mixing bowl and whisk together. Drizzle in 120ml of nice olive oil, whisk together. Taste, season with sea salt and freshly ground black pepper.

This makes the perfect summer lunch for friends, all you need to serve with it is a glass of chilled, crisp dry white wine, or two!

Summer Garden

Ingredients

Marinated goat's cheese

100g soft goat's cheese
½ teaspoon chopped herbs
1 garlic clove, sliced thinly
1 small chilli split down the middle
2 slices of lemon zest
200ml olive oil

Base

400g cooked peas, blitzed
and sieved
1 fat garlic clove (cooked and blitzed
with the peas)
3 sprigs mint leaves, finely chopped
1 tablespoon Greek yoghurt
Sea salt and white pepper to taste

Top

1 small fennel bulb, sliced on
a mandolin
1 medium cucumber, sliced with
a vegetable peeler – no seeds
4 tablespoons white wine vinegar
1 tablespoon maple syrup
1 flat teaspoon fennel seeds
1 heaped teaspoon chopped herbs
e.g. fennel, chives, parsley

Garnish

1 bunch thin asparagus-tips
blanched, stems cooked and puréed
4 radishes, trimmed and sliced
thinly
2 tablespoons blanched broad beans,
out of their skins
Edible flowers – chive, marigold,
heartsease, sprinkle of coriander
a few small green olives, some little
roasted tomatoes (see page 20)

Serves 6-8

What you do

1 Start by marinading the goat's
cheese. Divide the cheese into 16
mini portions, roll into balls and
place in a small sterilised jar. Mix
together the rest of the ingredients
with the olive oil and pour over the
cheese. Cover and pop in the fridge
for at least an hour, or overnight.

2 Prepare the base of the garden by
mixing together the pea, and garlic
purée, chopped mint and yoghurt.
Taste, and season accordingly. Pop a

sheet of cling film directly on to the purée and chill until needed – you can make this the day before, like the marinated cheese.

3 Mix together the sliced fennel and cucumber (to shred nicely, pile about 4 ribbons on top of each other and then cut into thin strips with a sharp knife) with the wine vinegar, syrup, fennel seeds and herbs, cover and pop in the fridge.

4 Prepare the garnish and place in bundles on a plate ready to serve.

5 To serve, spread the pea purée over the base of a large main course sized plate or 4-6 individual plates and smooth out with the back of a spoon. Top with a portion of the fennel and cucumber. Garnish with a mix of asparagus, radish and broad beans. Dot the marinated cheese between the veggies, drizzle with a little of the oil and finish with the edible flowers, coriander leaves, olives and roasted tomatoes. Serve with the Sardinian crisp bread (see page 52).

This is my pretty summer garden on a plate. Packed full of colour, great flavours and delicious shards of crisp Sardinian style bread to scoop up the yumminess.

Italian Crisp Bread

This recipe comes from Sardinia and is sometimes called "Carta di Musica" – Music Sheet. The rolled dough is so thin that you should be able to read a sheet of music through the rolled dough before baking. I sometimes use a pasta machine to make super thin sheets which are light, crisp and perfect for dipping and scooping.

Ingredients

240g bread flour

240g semolina flour

1 flat teaspoon sea salt

½ teaspoon baking powder

200-250ml warm water

1½ tablespoons olive oil

Serves 6-8

What you do

1 Combine the bread flour, semolina flour, sea salt and baking powder in a large bowl. Slowly mix in enough lukewarm water to form a moist, soft dough. Knead the dough in a bowl until it is no longer sticky. Then knead the dough on a lightly floured work surface until it is smooth, this should take about 15 minutes. Cover the dough with cling film and leave it to stand at room temperature for at least 20 minutes.

2 Preheat the oven to 220°C/ Fan 200°C/Gas 7. Very lightly dust 2 large baking sheets with flour. Divide the dough into 4 equal pieces. Pat 1 of the pieces into a disk shape, keeping the rest of the dough covered. Roll the disk out until it is around 13-inches around, lifting and turning often. Transfer the rolled dough to a baking sheet and bake until the edges begin to turn up and the bread is still malleable. This should take about 6 minutes.

Turn the bread over and bake until the bread bubbles in spots and is golden in places – about an extra 5 minutes.

3 Remove the dough from the oven, brush with olive oil and sprinkle with sea salt. Then return to the oven and bake for a further 3 minutes. When finished, cool on a rack and repeat for the remaining 3 pieces of dough.

4 You can also finish the bread with finely chopped rosemary, or my delicious flavoured oil.

Flavoured oil

50ml olive oil mixed with 1 finely grated garlic clove, 8 shredded basil leaves and ½ a teaspoon of grated lemon zest, brush over the crisp bread before returning to the oven for 5 minutes.

The addition of the flavoured oil gives the crisp bread a wonderful aromatic finish.

Provençal Tart

The essence of Provence is captured in this delicious tart; it's one of my favourites and I love serving it for lunch with a simple salad and a jar of marinated olives.

Ingredients

300g shortcrust pastry

Filling

1 rounded tablespoon Dijon mustard
3 tablespoons water
Fine sea salt
5 tablespoons extra virgin olive oil
4 medium white onions, peeled and
thinly sliced
1 bay leaf
6 roasted peppers
1 tablespoon fresh chopped Herbs
de Provence

Basil and Parmesan crumb

150g focaccia bread in cubes
1 fat garlic clove
8 stems basil, leaves only
2 heaped tablespoons grated
Parmesan
2 tablespoons olive oil

To finish

8 black olives

Serves 4-6

What you do

① Preheat the oven to 200°C/Fan 180°C/Gas 6. Divide the pastry into 4 portions, roll into balls and roll out to fit 4 tartlet tins – pre-buttered and floured. Prick the base of the tarts all over with a fork. Line with parchment paper, fill with baking beans and chill for 1 hour. Alternatively, line an 8" loose-bottom tart tin and prepare as above.

② Meanwhile, make the filling. Heat the water and oil together, add the onions and bay leaf and cook over a low heat until completely soft and just turning colour; they should not brown.

③ Bake the tart cases until lightly golden at the edges, about 15 minutes. Remove the paper and beans and lower the heat to 170°C/Fan 150°C/Gas 3 and cook until the pastry is dry to the touch.

④ Brush the inside of the tart all over with the Dijon mustard. Stir the herbs through the onions then pile into the cases. Lay the sweet roasted peppers on top.

5 For the basil and Parmesan crumb, place all the ingredients in a food processor and blitz until a crumb consistency is formed. Spoon over the peppers and spread evenly. Stud with black olives and bake in the oven for 15 minutes at 190°C/Fan 170°C/Gas 5.

6 Serve warm or at room temperature with a crisp green salad.

Shortcrust Pastry

This takes just a few minutes in a food processor and will make 2 x 8" tart bases or 1 x 12" tart. Put 500g plain flour into a processor bowl, add 250g chilled unsalted butter and briefly blitz together until the mixture looks like fine breadcrumbs. Add 50g finely grated Parmesan, ½ teaspoon cayenne pepper and 1 tablespoon of fresh thyme or rosemary leaves. Pulse briefly. Break in 2 medium eggs and pulse again to bring together into a dough. If it looks a little dry, add a teaspoon or 2 of cold water.

Use any leftover pastry to make 4 small tartlets or freeze it ready to use next time.

Spanakopita
Greek Spinach Pie

I can remember the first time I ate this in Chios, it was one of those moments you never forget. Total perfection from first bite to the last!

Ingredients

2 tablespoons olive oil

25g butter, plus a little extra for brushing the top

1 large onion, sliced thinly

2 large spring onions, chopped finely

1 large garlic clove, grated

700g spinach, washed and roughly chopped

¼ teaspoon grated nutmeg

200g feta cheese, crumbled

2 large free-range eggs, beaten

2 tablespoons chopped dill and parsley mixed

Sea salt and pepper to taste

5 large sheets of filo pastry cut in half to fit your tin (6 base layers, 4 top layers)

Serves 6-8

What you do

1 Heat the oven to 200°C/Fan 180°C/Gas 6.

2 To prepare the filling, heat 2 tablespoons of olive oil and the butter in a large frying pan and sauté the onion until soft, just turning golden. Add the spring onions and garlic and stir through, then add spinach and cook until wilted. Cool, then tip into a bowl (leaving behind any excess liquid from the spinach) and mix in the nutmeg, feta, eggs, and chopped herbs, season to your taste.

3 To assemble, you will need a 25cm nonstick baking pan, it can be round or rectangular, even a foil or baking tin is perfect. Brush the base with olive oil and put the first sheet of filo in the tin (let the edges hang over the sides) and brush with olive oil. Repeat until you have used 6 sheets. Spoon in the filling, then layer up 4 sheets of filo brushing with olive oil in-between to form the

top. Trim away any excess filo from the edges and tuck in neatly.

④ Brush the top with a little melted butter, then take a sharp knife and cut equally spaced lines diagonally, then cut the other way to create diamond shapes. Bake in preheated oven for 40-60 minutes until the spanakopita is crisp and golden. Leave to cool down for 10-15 minutes before cutting into pieces.

So good served with a simple plate of sliced sun-ripened tomatoes. Overlap the slices, drizzle with good olive oil, sprinkle with a little sea salt, a few twists of black pepper and dot with a few black olives if you like. Perfect!

Spiced Crab Tart

I remember one of Andrew Lloyd Weber's guests sending a postcard of thanks, on which his last words were "Still dreaming of that crab tart!" Well here it is!

Ingredients

350g shortcrust pastry
(½ quantity of recipe on page 59)

25g butter

2 teaspoons olive oil

1 small onion, very finely chopped

1 fat garlic clove, finely grated
with sea salt to make a paste

1 small chilli, deseeded and chopped
finely

1 small anchovy, pasted and mixed
with the garlic

1 teaspoon lemon juice

1 heaped teaspoon curry powder
(optional)

150ml double cream

4 large free-range eggs

1 tablespoon chopped coriander or
parsley

300g mixed crab meat – brown and
white

1 flat teaspoon of sea salt

¼ teaspoon black pepper

Serves 4-6

What you do

1 First, lightly butter and flour a 9"/20cm loose-bottom tart tin. Flour a patch of your work surface and your rolling pin. Roll out the pastry evenly to a thin biscuit thickness. Use your rolling pin to pick up the pastry, carefully guide it into the tin and gently ease it into the edge at the base. Press gently into place all the way around, and then trim off the excess pastry. Prick the base evenly all over with a fork.

2 Set your oven to 200°C/Fan 180°C/Gas 6, line the tart with baking parchment and fill with baking beans. Bake for around 15 minutes, or until it is lightly golden at the edges. Then remove the paper and baking beans, reduce the heat to 150°C/Fan 130°C/Gas 3 then for a further 10-12 minutes until dry to the touch in the middle.

3 To make the filling, heat the butter with 2 teaspoons of olive oil, add the onion and cook gently until

soft and lightly golden. Stir in the garlic, chilli, anchovy, lemon juice, curry powder (if using) and cook for about a minute, then stir in the cream, let it bubble together for a minute, then remove from the heat and leave to cool slightly.

4 Beat the eggs together in a mixing bowl and pour in the spicy cream, the coriander or parsley and crab meat. Season with 1 flat teaspoon of sea salt and a ¼ teaspoon of black pepper. Mix well and pour into the prepared cooked pastry shell. Place on a baking sheet and bake at 180°C/Fan 160°C/Gas 4 until set – about 30 minutes..

5 Remove from the oven and cool slightly before removing it from the tin.

6 Serve warm or cold with a lovely summer leaf salad.

This tart is so deliciously rich, it just needs a simple mix of summer salad leaves dressed with a good vinaigrette to accompany it.

Stuffed Giant Pasta Shells with Roasted Tomato and Red Pepper Sauce

Ingredients

Stuffed pasta shells

2 tablespoons olive oil

1 small onion, finely diced

1 fat garlic clove, finely grated with sea salt to make a paste

4 tablespoons water

2 tablespoons white wine

450g cooked cannellini or butter beans

½ teaspoon grated lemon zest

2 heaped tablespoons crème fraiche

16 cooked giant pasta shells

Sauce

2 medium roasted red peppers

4 medium roasted tomatoes

1 teaspoon white wine vinegar

¼ teaspoon sugar

2 tablespoons crème fraiche

To finish

2 tablespoons fresh pesto (see page 24)

A couple of handfuls of rocket leaves

Serves 4

What you do

1 To make the filling, heat the olive oil in a frying pan. Add the chopped onion and stir through and sauté gently for 10 minutes. Add the garlic and stir through, add 4 tablespoons of water and turn the heat down so the onions are simmering gently.

2 When the onions are soft and sticky in consistency, add the wine and boil for 30 seconds to cook off the alcohol, then add the beans, lemon zest and créme fraiche. Bubble together, stirring occasionally until thickened. Tip into a measuring jug and blitz to a smooth purée using a stick blender, taste and season accordingly. Cover and leave to cool.

3 Next, make the sauce. Chop up the roasted peppers and tomatoes and pop into a jug. Add the other ingredients and blitz with a stick

blender to make a smooth sauce. For an ultra-smooth finish, you can push the sauce through a sieve. Taste and season accordingly.

4 To serve, fill the pasta shells with the cooled bean filling (it should be room temperature and not straight from the fridge). Spoon some of the red pepper sauce onto serving plates, top with the pasta shells and finish with a drizzle of pesto and a scattering of rocket leaves.

Something a little different for a lunch together with friends, and you can make all the elements in advance and then bring them together easily in no time at all.

Tagliatelle with Summer Herb Butter, Peas and Beans

Making pasta is easier than you may think and it's such good fun putting it through the pasta rollers, or even rolling it by hand. Once you have a silky smooth dough, the possibilities are endless. Making tagliatelle is simple and it's a good one to start with, all you need is a delicious sauce and you have a lovely lunch or supper.

Ingredients

Fresh pasta

340g 00 flour
160g semolina flour
Large pinch of fine sea salt
3 large free-range eggs and 2 or 3
egg yolks, at room temperature,
lightly beaten (if the mixture
doesn't come together with 2 yolks,
add the third)

Sauce

75g butter
1 garlic clove, grated
2 wide strips lemon zest cut into
fine strips
100g petit pois
100g broad beans
100g French beans

To finish

A handful of fresh basil leaves
1 heaped tablespoon grated
Parmesan
4 slices Parma ham, grilled until
crisp

Serves 4

What you do

1 Mix the flours together and tip
out onto your surface, sprinkle with
the salt and mix in. Make a large
well in the middle and pour in two
thirds of the beaten eggs. Using
your fingertips in a circular motion,
gradually stir in the flour until you
have a soft dough. Add more egg if
needed. Knead for about 10 minutes
until smooth and the dough springs
back when poked. Divide into two
and wrap in a damp cloth. Leave to
rest for about an hour.

2 To roll out using a pasta
machine, unwrap one portion of
the dough and place on a floured
surface, flatten into a rectangle and
then pass through a pasta roller at
the largest setting (0). Pass through
twice on each setting finishing on
number 6, then cut into tagliatelle.
If your pasta machine doesn't
have an attachment for this then
do it by hand. Liberally flour the
sheet of rolled pasta, loosely roll

up quickly and cut along the roll to the thickness of tagliatelle. Unravel quickly, sprinkle with flour and set aside. Repeat with the second piece of dough.

3 If you don't have a pasta machine, divide the dough into 4 portions, work on one at a time, moulding it into a rectangle and then roll out until ultra thin. You should be able to see the palm of your hand clearly through the dough. Liberally flour the surface of the sheet of pasta roll it up quickly and loosely, cut into tagliatelle widths, unravel and then proceed to cook.

4 Bring a large saucepan of salted water to the boil. Add the pasta and cook for 4 minutes until 'al dente'. Drain (reserve a ladle of the cooking water for the sauce). To finish, melt the butter in the large pasta pan, add the garlic and lemon zest and cook for a minute. Stir in the peas, broad and French beans, add the cooked tagliatelle and mix

together. Pour in the reserved cooking water and continue cooking gently for 5 minutes. Remove from the heat, break in the basil, stir in the Parmesan quickly and serve in warm bowls. Top with a slice of crisp Parma ham.

Crisp Parma Ham

Line a baking sheet with foil and brush lightly with olive oil. Lay 4 slices of Parma ham on top and then cover with another lightly oiled sheet of foil and then top with another baking sheet and press together. Bake in a preheated oven 200°C/Fan 180°C/Gas 6 and bake for 15 minutes, remove and lift off the top baking sheet and foil.

The Parma ham should be golden and slightly crisp at the edges, it may need a further 5-7 minutes depending on the thickness. Remove and lift the slices on to kitchen paper to absorb the excess oil. The ham will crisp up further as it cools.

Greek Salad

This is the perfect salad for enjoying outside in the sunshine. It is really delicious on its own, but I also like it served with roasted meat such as pork or chicken, wrapped up together in a soft flat bread.

Ingredients

1 large cucumber or 400g trimmed and cubed watermelon

1 small red onion

8 medium tomatoes – sun ripe or slow-roasted

4 tablespoons Greek Kalamata olives

A few mint leaves

200g Greek feta cheese

Sea salt and black pepper to taste

A good sprinkle of dried oregano

Greek olive oil to finish

Serves 4

What you do

1 Peel the cucumber, cut into quarters lengthways, then each piece in half and slice away the seeds. Cut into large bite size pieces and place in a mixing bowl. If using watermelon, make sure all the seeds are removed.

2 Peel and thinly slice the red onion then place in a bowl of cold water for 10 minutes to mellow the flavour.

3 Cut the tomatoes into chunks and add to the cucumber, sprinkle with a little sea salt, pepper and oregano, a drizzle of olive oil and mix together.

4 Break in the mint leaves and add the olives, tip into a serving bowl, top with the feta in one piece, sprinkle with oregano and black pepper and finish with a good drizzle of olive oil. Serve on its own with crusty bread, or with just about anything else, especially roasted, grilled or barbecued meats and fish.

The ripeness of the tomatoes are key to this salad. I like to give them a little extra attention by giving them a sprinkle of sea salt and sugar and a few twists of black pepper before mixing with the other ingredients. Good quality Kalamata olives and feta cheese are worth seeking out. I love a visit to the legendary Wally's Delicatessen in Cardiff for such ingredients, it's everything a great deli should be and more.

St. Jean Seafood with Pastis

I love this simple summer one-pot wonder, it's so reminiscent of the food I would eat at the local restaurant in St. Jean. The touch of Pastis together with local herbs is just heavenly.

Ingredients

Broth base

1kg white fish heads and bones

1 teaspoon sea salt, 4 peppercorns, 1 bay leaf, 1 large chopped carrot, 1 onion, 1 celery stick, plus 3 stems thyme and parsley

1 litre water

100ml white wine

The one-pot wonder!

4 tablespoons olive oil

2 medium onions, finely chopped

5 fat garlic cloves, finely grated

3 carrots, chopped

2 celery sticks, chopped

1 fennel bulb, chopped

250g baby plum or beef tomatoes, deseeded and chopped

1 tablespoon crushed fennel seeds

2 sprigs thyme

A good pinch of saffron strands

400g chunks of white fish fillets – monk, hake, cod

1kg clams/cockles and mussels, cleaned

A dash of Pernod

To serve

4 slices sourdough bread

Olive oil for frying

1 small bunch mixed herbs – parsley, fennel, chives

Rouille

1 large garlic clove, grated

½ large roasted red pepper

1 medium free-range egg yolk

1 teaspoon lemon juice

Pinch saffron threads soaked in a teaspoon hot water

240ml olive oil

Sea salt to taste

Pinch black pepper

Serves 4-6

What you do

1 Make a simple broth from the fish heads and bones: cover them with the water and wine, add in the other ingredients, bring to the boil and simmer for 20 minutes, skimming off any foam. Strain, discarding the solids and set aside.

2 Next, prepare the yummy serving toasts and rouille. Fry the bread slices in the olive oil until golden on both sides and drain on kitchen paper, set aside. For the rouille, use the bowl of a food processor to combine the garlic, red pepper, egg yolk, lemon juice, and saffron. Pulse until smooth, then slowly drizzle in the oil and process continuously until the mixture thickens. Season with salt and pepper to taste, set aside.

3 For the main dish, heat the olive oil in a large pan and add the vegetables, crushed fennel seeds, thyme, saffron and then the broth. Bring to the boil and simmer until the vegetables are soft. Add the fish and shellfish and cook, covered, for about five minutes or until the shellfish open (discard anything that doesn't open). Finish with a dash of Pernod and season with salt and pepper.

4 Ladle into warmed bowls, finish with the chopped herbs. Serve with the toasts and delicious Rouille.

A good dry white wine is good with this dish, but to be honest, I love pastis on the rocks with mine. It would always be my tipple at the end of a busy day in the kitchen and mark the time to unwind nicely.

Seafood
Plate

At first glance this recipe may look a little involved, but all the elements are easy to make and can be done in advance. The finished dish is a real treat for seafood lovers.

Ingredients

Base

1 tablespoon olive oil
1 large leek, trimmed and shredded
¼ teaspoon sea salt and a little pepper
1 tablespoon lemon juice
100g trimmed samphire
1 dessertspoon chopped parsley

Crab and brown shrimp bon bons

150g white crab meat
100g brown shrimp
50g fine soft breadcrumbs
1 free-range egg yolk
1 teaspoon chopped chives
½ teaspoon lemon zest
2 teaspoons lemon juice
Sea salt and white pepper
For dipping: flour, beaten free-range egg and panko breadcrumbs

Laver gnocchi

100g laverbread
1 garlic clove, grated
2 tablespoons rolled oats
1 teaspoon sesame seeds

1 teaspoon lemon juice
¼ teaspoon black pepper
1 tablespoon chopped parsley
Sunflower oil for frying

The fish

1 tablespoon olive oil
25g butter
2 thick slices of bacon
2 handfuls of live cockles
4 x 175g salmon, sewin, trout or bass fillets
2 tablespoons lime juice
1 tablespoon olive oil
1 teaspoon smoked or plain sea salt
Freshly ground black pepper
1 tablespoon chopped mixed herbs e.g. parsley, chives, dill
Sunflower oil for frying
Vinaigrette (see page 47)

Serves 4

What you do

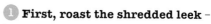 **First, roast the shredded leek** – line a baking sheet with parchment paper, spread the leeks over, drizzle with the olive oil and season with salt and pepper. Roast until golden

– you will have to mix the leeks through a couple of times during cooking to make sure they cook evenly – this should take about 12-15 minutes. Add the samphire for last 5 minutes of cooking, The leeks should be golden at the tips and soft in the middle. Remove and dress with lemon juice and parsley.

2 **Make the bon bons** – place all the ingredients in a food processor (apart from the dipping ingredients) and pulse to combine. Form into 12 little balls and then flour, egg and breadcrumb them. Keep in the fridge until needed.

3 **Make the gnocchi** – mix together the laverbread, garlic, oats, sesame seeds, lemon juice, pepper and parsley in a bowl. Mix well and divide into 16 little balls and then flatten into discs. Chill until ready to cook.

4 **To cook the fish** – cut the bacon into fine strips. Heat the olive oil with the butter in a large non-stick pan and fry the bacon until lightly

golden, add the cockles and cook with a lid on until open. Remove and keep warm. Reheat the pan and quickly mix together the salt, pepper, lime juice, olive oil and herbs, spread half over the fish skin, place skin side down (it should sizzle loudly), keep them sizzling, but not burning. Spread the remaining herb mix over the flesh of the fillets. When the skin is crisp and golden underneath, use a palette knife to carefully turn the fillets over. Finish cooking the fish through (aprox 3-6 mins), remove from heat and keep warm in the pan.

5 Meanwhile, heat another pan and shallow fry the gnocchi and the bon bons until lightly golden. Drain on kitchen paper. Keep warm in a low heated oven.

6 **To assemble the dish** – divide the leeks and samphire between 4 plates, spread out and place the fish in the centre. Dot the gnocchi, bon bons, bacon and cockles to garnish. Drizzle over a little of the the vinaigrette dressing to finish.

Paella

Ingredients

Base

12 medium raw tiger prawns in their shells

130ml olive oil

4 good sized free-range chicken thighs on the bone

4 fat garlic cloves, finely grated with sea salt to make a paste

1L water

1 tablespoon Marigold Swiss vegetable powder

1 large onion, peeled and finely diced

2 teaspoons smoked paprika

400g chopped tomatoes, cherry and Santa have great flavour

100ml dry white wine

½ teaspoon saffron soaked in 2 tablespoons hot water

300g Calasparra or other short-grain rice

250g beans, e.g. broad beans or lovely summer peas

250g mussels, scrubbed and de-bearded

100g live cockles (optional)

1 small bunch of flat-leaf parsley, chopped

1 lemon, cut into wedges to serve

Serves 4

What you do

① First, make the stock. Remove the heads and shells from 8 of the prawns, use the remaining 4 as the garnish. Heat 2 tablespoons of the oil in a pan, add the prawn heads and shells and sauté until they turn pink and start to turn golden. Stir in one of the pasted garlic cloves and cook for 30 seconds. Pour in the water, add the vegetable powder and bring to the boil, reduce the heat and simmer for 20 minutes then strain, ready to use.

② To start the paella, heat the remaining olive oil in a 26cm paella pan or a similar sized wide pan.

Add the chicken thighs and sauté for about five minutes until slightly browned, season with sea salt and black pepper.

3 Add the onion and garlic and cook until softened. This bit is important, so take it slowly, add a little water and cover with foil so the onion steams, then remove and cook off the moisture until the onions become sticky. Stir in the smoked paprika and cook for one minute, then add the tomatoes and wine; increase the heat and simmer for about 15 minutes until the mixture is paste-like and concentrated.

4 Stir in the rice, coating the grains well with the juices, followed by the beans. Pour in 800ml of the stock and the saffron with soaking water. Simmer for 20 minutes then arrange the prawns, mussels and cockles on top of the rice, burying them slightly but don't stir! Arrange the whole prawns on top. Cover with foil and cook for about 10-12 minutes. The mussels and cockles

should be open (discard any that don't) and the prawns should be pink. If the rice looks a little thirsty, stir in some of the leftover stock to give a rich and creamy finish.

5 Leave to stand for at least 10 minutes before serving. Finish with chopped parsley and lemon wedges.

This is the perfect food for an al fresco gathering, it's such sociable food that people can just tuck into.

Slow-Roasted Welsh Lamb

Ingredients

Leg of Welsh lamb, around 2.5kg

Rub

1 rounded teaspoon garlic granules

1 teaspoon dried oregano or marjoram

1 tablespoon grated lemon zest

1 tablespoon olive oil

1 rounded teaspoon sea salt

½ teaspoon ground black pepper

Glaze

6 tablespoons lemon juice

8 tablespoons orange juice

1 lavender flower

4 tablespoons runny honey

To finish

1 dessertspoon fresh chopped oregano

Serves 6-8

What you do

1 First, make a rub for the lamb. Mix together all the ingredients and rub all over the lamb, cover and leave for at least an hour, or overnight in the fridge.

2 Make the glaze in advance – put everything in a small saucepan and boil until the liquid thickens slightly like a syrup.

3 Make sure the lamb is at room temperature before you cook it. Pre-heat the barbecue for indirect heat at approximately 200°C, or set your oven to 200°C/Fan 180°C/Gas 6.

4 **If using a charcoal barbecue**, place the lamb directly in the middle of the grid and place the lid back on and cook for 20 minutes, then lower the temperature by partially closing the vents below and on the top until it reaches 160°C. Cook for about 1 hour or until the internal temperature of the meat reaches between 60°C-65°C (use a meat thermometer).

5 During the last 15 minutes, baste half the glaze all over the lamb, BBQ for 10 minutes then brush the remaining glaze on to finish cooking. Then remove from the heat, cover and rest for 15 minutes before carving.

6 **Alternatively, roast in the oven** for 20 minutes at 220°C/Fan 200°C/Gas 7, then reduce the heat to 160°C/Fan 140°C/Gas 3 and cook for 1 hour and 15 minutes, or until the internal temperature of the lamb is between 60°C-65°C (use a meat thermometer). Brush with half the glaze, cook for another 10 minutes then brush on the remaining glaze, remove from the heat, cover and rest for 15 minutes.

7 Sprinkle with the fresh chopped oregano and carve.

8 Serve with tzatziki, tapenade and skordalia dipping sauces (page 98).

This is my favourite time of year to eat lamb. I find it has a fuller flavour and slow cooking really brings out all its qualities. The sauces are stunning and you can use them to add pizzazz to any feast.

Tzatziki, Tapenade and Skordalia

These dipping sauces really capture the flavours of the Mediterranean and go well with so many dishes. Use them to create a mezze and scoop up with crisp or flat breads; or serve alongside rich, roasted meats, griddled fish and sticky roasted vegetables. They are also ideal to pack up in jars and take on a picnic.

Tzatziki

Ingredients

1 large cucumber, peeled and grated
(excluding seeds)
½ teaspoon sea salt
500ml Greek yoghurt
2 fat garlic cloves, grated
Pinch of pepper
1 dessertspoon chopped dill
1 tablespoon chopped mint
1 dessertspoon wine vinegar

Serves 4-6

What you do

1 To make the tzatziki, place the cucumber in a sieve over a bowl, sprinkle with the salt and strain for 20 minutes. Squeeze out the excess liquid and place the cucumber in a bowl.

2 Add the yoghurt and stir in the garlic, dill, mint and vinegar. Cover and chill until needed.

Tapenade

Ingredients

1 fat garlic clove, crushed
2 tablespoons lemon juice
3 tablespoons capers, chopped
6 anchovy fillets, chopped
250g good black olives, pitted and chopped
Small bunch fresh parsley, chopped
½ teaspoon sea salt
¼ teaspoon freshly ground black pepper
2-4 tablespoons extra virgin olive oil

Serves 4-6

What you do

1 To make a rough textured tapenade, simply mix all the ingredients together, adding enough olive oil to form a paste.

2 For a smoother texture, tip the garlic, lemon juice, capers and anchovy into a food processor and

process for about 10 seconds. Add the olives and parsley and enough olive oil to make a smooth paste.

Skordalia

Ingredients

250g red skinned potatoes, washed
Sea salt
4 large garlic cloves
2 tablespoons lemon juice
1 tablespoon white wine vinegar
90g whole blanched almonds
1 level teaspoon sea salt
60ml olive oil
60ml water

Serves 4-6

What you do

1 Boil the potatoes in their skins in plenty of salted water.

2 Once the potatoes are soft through, remove from the pan and cool slightly. Peel away the skins, cut into large chunks and pass through a potato ricer directly into a mixing bowl. Alternatively, use a potato masher and make sure there are no lumps.

3 Paste the garlic with the flat of a chopping knife. To do this, bash the garlic until flat, sprinkle with the sea salt and work into the garlic. Drag the garlic towards you under the knife repeatedly until it turns to a paste.

4 In a food processor, combine the garlic, almonds, olive oil and purée into a paste. Mix this into the potatoes until incorporated, then mix in 1 flat teaspoon of sea salt, the water, lemon juice, and vinegar and season with pepper, to taste. Serve.

Summer
Ballotine
of Chicken

Ingredients

1 large free-range chicken, all bones removed and in one piece. (Ask your butcher to do this, or challenge yourself and follow a YouTube "How to" video.)

Sea salt and black pepper

A few stems of thyme

3 bay leaves

Olive oil for drizzling

2 chicken breasts

4 slices of Parma ham

200g fresh pesto
(see page 24)

75g breadcrumbs

1 sheet baking parchment

1 large sheet of thick foil

Serves 4-6

What you do

1 Preheat the oven to 190°C/ Fan 170°C/Gas 5.

2 Lay the sheet of foil on your work top, place the baking parchment sheet in the centre and sprinkle with sea salt and pepper. Scatter the thyme sprigs along the centre and space the bay leaves along the middle.

3 Lay the whole chicken on top along the centre, skin side down and open out completely. Season well with sea salt and pepper.

4 Mix the pesto and breadcrumbs together and spoon half along the centre of the chicken. Lay the slices of Parma ham along the middle and lay the chicken breasts end to end on top. Spoon the remaining pesto on top of the chicken breasts – all this filling should create a cylinder shape, replacing the removed rib cage.

5 Now you need to roll the chicken up. Pull the baking parchment to the edge of the foil near you, pull it up and over, rolling the chicken forward, like a Swiss Roll. Ease the

rolled chicken and paper back to the edge of the foil, you need to tuck in the ends of the chicken, tuck the skin underneath at each end. Now pick up the edge of the foil and roll forward again, this time all the way until tightly wrapped. Twist each end of the foil tightly to create a big cracker shape. Place in a roasting tin and cook for 20 minutes per 450g.

6 For the last 15 minutes of cooking time, cut away the foil and paper, make sure the join is under the chicken, baste and then drain off the cooking juices into a small pan. Return the chicken to the oven, increase the heat to 220°C/ Fan 200°C/Gas 7 and roast for 15 minutes until the chicken is crisp and golden. Rest for 15-20 minutes before carving, or eat cold.

Note: You can add 100ml of white wine to the cooking juices and boil together to make a delicious full-flavoured sauce.

7 Serve with a fresh green salad and slow-roasted tomatoes.

Something a little special that takes time to prepare. It's really popular at the School as there is a real sense of achievement in preparing and cooking this dish.

Porchetta

This is perfect for a large supper party and there really is little effort involved. Just buy good quality pork and let the marinade do its work, together with slow cooking for delicious results.

Ingredients

1 x rectangular piece of boneless pork belly – skin left on and a piece of pork loin of roughly the right size to be rolled up inside (how much each piece weighs depends on the shape, but aim for a total weight of about 3.5-4kg)

1 tablespoon fennel seeds

1 teaspoon chipotle dried chilli flakes

1 rounded tablespoon sea salt flakes

20 fat garlic cloves, peeled and crushed

2 tablespoons chopped fresh rosemary and thyme leaves

2 tablespoons olive oil

200ml white wine

6 sprigs rosemary

Serves 10-12

What you do

1 Heat a small pan and add the fennel seeds and chilli flakes, lightly toast until aromatic and then tip into a small blender or pestle and mortar. Add the garlic, chopped rosemary, thyme, olive oil and wine. Blitz together to form a paste.

2 Place the pork belly on a clean, flat surface, score the flesh, then rub the paste into the meat with your hands. Lay the sprigs of rosemary down the middle. Sit the loin long-side parallel to the shorter side of the belly, and then roll up tightly.

3 Tie up tightly with butcher's string at about 5cm intervals, and leave to sit, uncovered in the fridge, for at least 8 hours. Bring back to room temperature before cooking.

4 Heat the oven to 160°C/Fan 140°C/Gas 3.

5 Pat the meat as dry as possible with kitchen paper and put on a

rack in a roasting tray. Roast for approximately 4 hours, then turn the oven up to 220°C/Fan 200°C/Gas 7 and roast for 30 minutes, until the skin is crisp and golden. Remove and rest the pork for 20 minutes before carving.

6 Alternatively cook the porchetta on the BBQ, set for indirect cooking. Place in the centre of the grill and cook at 160°C, adjust the vents to achieve the temperature, cook for approximately 4 hours – the internal temperature of the meat (use a meat thermometer) should reach 70°C, then top up the baskets with a further ½ chimney of lit coals, open the vents full so the temperature goes up to 200°C-220°C to finish the cooking and crisp up the skin. Remove from the heat and rest for 20 minutes before carving.

7 Slice and serve with green olive salsa.

Green olive salsa

1 fat garlic clove, finely grated with sea salt to make a paste

150g green olives

1 tablespoon capers

2 tablespoons chopped parsley

1 teaspoon grated lemon zest

1 tablespoon lemon juice

1 salted anchovy (optional)

Black pepper to taste.

What you do

1 Mix everything together and serve. Or make ahead and cover, keep in the fridge for up to 3 days.

Tagliata

Every now and then I really fancy a steak and this is the way I always cook it. No rich sauces, just a few little touches and you're done!

Ingredients

4 x 200g thick Welsh sirloin or rib eye steaks

4 tablespoons olive oil

Sea salt and black pepper

To finish

50g salted butter

1 fat garlic clove, sliced super thin

4 wide strips lemon zest, cut into thin matchsticks

4 lemon wedges

4 sprigs rosemary, chopped, a few basil leaves, torn

Salt and pepper

To serve

4 small handfuls rocket

50g Parmesan shavings

Serves 2 or 4 small starter plates

What you do

1 Heat a skillet pan.

2 Make sure the steaks are at room temperature. Rub the steaks with the olive oil and season well with sea salt and fresh ground black pepper.

3 Sear the steaks in the pan to seal both sides to give a colourful crust, reduce the heat to low-medium and cook your steak to your liking. Use the muscle on your hand below your thumb to measure how cooked the steak is. The index finger to thumb is similar to how a rare steak feels when prodded. As you try with each finger in succession, you will feel the muscle tightening up, as will the steak as it cooks, moving along from medium to well done.

4 When you are happy, remove the steak from the pan to rest. Add the butter, garlic and lemon zest to the pan and cook until lightly golden. Take off the heat and add the herbs – be careful not to burn the butter.

⑤ Let the steaks rest for 5 minutes, then cut into slices. Tip any juices back into the pan and mix with the other ingredients.

⑥ Plate the steak slices, pour the pan juices, lemon and garlic over the top. Finish with rocket and Parmesan.

Serve with the lemon wedges and little roasted potatoes, plain crisp salad and roasted tomatoes are really good with this.

Spiced Chicken Patties with Preserved Lemon and Coriander

If you like a little spice, then these hit the spot. I love serving them with soft flat breads, shredded salad and tzatziki.

Ingredients

Olive oil

1 large red onion, finely chopped

2 fat garlic cloves, grated

1 rounded teaspoon sea salt

¼ teaspoon black pepper

2 preserved lemons, pips removed and chopped

1 teaspoon ground cumin

1 small bunch coriander, chopped

500g boneless chicken thighs/legs

1 medium free-range egg

25g pistachios

100g fresh breadcrumbs

Serves 4

What you do

1 Place the onion, garlic, salt, pepper, preserved lemon, cumin, coriander and pistachios in a food processor, blitz to break down. Cut the chicken into small cubes, add to the processor with the egg, blitz to break down and combine with all the other ingredients. Remove the mixture and place in a mixing bowl, stir in the breadcrumbs, wet your hands and divide the mixture into 4 portions and shape into patties and flatten slightly.

2 Pour a little light olive oil into a large frying pan and heat. When hot, add the patties and cook until brown on each side, this should take a minute on each side. Then turn the heat down and cook for a further 4 minutes on each side.

3 Check they are cooked through.

4 Serve with tzatziki (see page 100) and a mixed salad.

Note

You can make the flavouring mixture into a paste with the addition of some olive oil to loosen it. Spread all over a free-range chicken and roast 20 minutes per 400g at 180°C/Fan 160°C/Gas 4, baste at intervals. Rest, loosely covered with foil for 20 minutes before shredding up and drizzling with the delicious juices. Serve with flat breads, salad and the tzatziki.

Flat Breads

250g strong flour

½ teaspoon fine sea salt

½ teaspoon instant dried yeast

½ teaspoon honey

160ml warm water

1 tablespoon sunflower oil, plus extra for rolling

Makes 6

What you do

1 Mix the flour and salt in a bowl. Stir in the instant yeast and make a deep well in the centre, add the warm water, honey and sunflower oil and mix together to create a smooth, stretchy dough. Lightly oil your work surface and throw the dough so it elongates away from you when it hits the surface. Roll it back towards you into a ball and repeat about 20 times. The dough will become smoother and firmer. Place the dough in a lightly oiled bowl and cover with a cloth. Leave until doubled in size. Oil your work surface, tip out the dough and divide into 6 portions, knead each of them lightly. Leave for 10 minutes. In the meantime heat up a large, heavy-based pan.

2 Lightly flour your work surface and roll out each dough ball to the size of a side plate. Lightly oil the pan and cook the flat breads one at a time. Cook over a low heat until golden then turn over and repeat the other side. Repeat and cook the rest of the breads.

Hot Smoked Barbecued Gammon with Mango and Chilli Glaze

Ingredients

1 piece of gammon, approximately 2.5kg

Pre-rub

1 teaspoon sea salt

½ teaspoon black pepper

1 teaspoon mustard powder

1 teaspoon sweet paprika

½ teaspoon chilli powder

Glaze

2 large soft mangoes, de-stoned and the flesh chopped

100ml maple syrup

50g muscovado sugar

1 flat teaspoon chipotle chilli paste

¼ teaspoon allspice

Smoking

Cherry or apple wood chips

Serves 8

What you do

1 First, make the glaze. Put everything into a saucepan, bring to the boil, reduce the heat and simmer until thickened and sticky.

2 Soak two handfuls of cherry or apple wood chips for 15 minutes.

3 Set your BBQ for indirect cooking with ½ a chimney of hot charcoals. Open all the vents and allow to come to 200°C.

4 If using an oven, set the temperature at 200°C/Fan 180°C/Gas 6.

5 Using a sharp knife, remove the skin from the gammon, score the fat into diamonds by running the knife from one corner to the opposite one, then repeat going from the other corner.

6 Mix together the pre-rub ingredients and rub into the fat.

7 Place in the centre of the BBQ, add a handful of soaked wood chips

to each basket of coals. Place the lid on and smoke for 15 minutes. Then brush with ½ the glaze and place the lid on, cook for 30 minutes. Repeat with the remaining glaze and cook for a further 30 minutes. Reduce the heat slightly to 170°C-180°C if the skin gets too dark.

8 Do the same if you are cooking the gammon in the oven at 200°C/Fan 180°C/Gas 6. Remove and rest the gammon for 15 minutes before carving.

9 Serve with summer slaw.

Summer slaw

1 small summer cabbage, shredded finely

½ small red onion, finely shredded

100g mange tout or French beans, shredded

1 small fennel bulb, shredded

1 ripe mango, chopped

100ml fresh squeezed orange juice

2 tablespoons lemon juice

1 tablespoon wine vinegar

1 teaspoon Dijon mustard

1 teaspoon maple syrup

1 tablespoon parsley, chopped

What you do

1 Pre-soak the red onion in cold water for 15 minutes.

2 Mix together the cabbage, red onion, mange tout or French beans, fennel and mango.

3 In a bowl, mix the orange juice, lemon juice, wine vinegar, mustard, syrup and parsley.

4 Tip the dressing into the vegetables, mix through and serve.

This is so delicious hot smoked on a BBQ, but you can also roast it conventionally and still achieve a wonderful sticky glazed finish.

Chicken Provençal

You may think this is a bit dated, but it is a real classic, and made with a little attention and love, it can be something really special.

Ingredients

2 tablespoons olive oil

25g butter

8 large chicken thighs, skin on

2 medium onions, thinly sliced

2 sweet peppers, deseeded and sliced thinly

3 fat garlic cloves, finely grated with sea salt to make a paste

2 tablespoons Provençal herbs

Sea salt and black pepper

300ml passata sauce

200ml white wine – something you would drink!

Few black or green olives (optional)

To finish

2 tablespoons fresh parsley, chopped

Hot garlic bread to serve

Serves 4

What you do

1 Heat the oil and butter together in a frying pan, add the chicken skin side down, cook in 2 batches to brown evenly. Place the chicken in a casserole dish or a chef pan with lid. Add the onions to the frying pan together with the peppers, add 100ml water and sauté until soft. Remove the lid and cook off the moisture so everything goes light brown and sticky.

2 Stir in the garlic and herbs and cook for a couple of minutes. Now add the seasoning, start with 1 flat teaspoon sea salt and $1/8$ teaspoon pepper, you can add more later if needed. Add the onion mixture to the chicken. Bring the casserole up to heat and pour in the passata and wine. Bring to the boil and then reduce to a slow simmer, cover and cook for about an hour – you can add a few black or green olives if you like.

③ Take out the chicken thighs and turn the heat up under the juices to cook them down into a sauce consistency. Plate the chicken, pour over the sauce, sprinkle with the chopped parsley and serve with hot garlic bread. Yum!

Garlic Bread

8 slices of baguette, the thickness of your thumb

100g salted butter, softened

2 fat garlic cloves, grated finely

1 tablespoon parsley, chopped

① Place the slices of bread on a baking sheet.

② Mix together the butter, garlic and parsley. Spread over the tops of the bread and bake in the oven at 200°C/Fan 180°C/Gas 6 and cook until golden at the edges, about 15 minutes.

③ Remove from the oven and arrange around the edge of the Chicken Provençal dish, with half of the bread in the sauce, so it soaks it up. It's a heavenly mix of soft and crisp with loads of flavour!

This dish is one of those that matures beautifully in flavour if left for 24-48 hours, then reheated gently.

Summer Pudding with Rose and Cassis

Ingredients

850g mixed red/black fruits e.g. raspberries, blackcurrants, good strawberries, a few redcurrants

10-12 slices firm, good quality white bread

3 rounded tablespoons sugar

2 tablespoons water

1 tablespoon cassis

½ teaspoon rose essence

Glaze

150g frozen red/black fruits

3 tablespoons sugar

4 tablespoons water

2 tablespoon cassis

Serves 6-8

What you do

1 Prepare the fruit – pull the redcurrants from their stems then put them, with the raspberries, in a stainless-steel saucepan over a low heat. Taste the fruit for sweetness and add the sugar accordingly. For normal, sweet raspberries and slightly tart redcurrants, add 3 tablespoons or so of sugar. Sometimes you may need slightly less or more. Pour in the water.

2 The currants will start to burst and give out their juice. They need no longer than three or four minutes at a gentle simmer. The fruit should be shiny and there should be plenty of deep-coloured juice in the pan. Turn off the heat and stir in the cassis and rose essence.

3 Cut the crusts off the bread. Set 1 slice aside for the base, then cut the rest into three long fingers. Using a glass or cup as a template, cut a disc of bread from the reserved slice, dip into the fruit juice and push in to the base of a 2 pint pudding basin.

4 Line the inside of the basin with the strips of bread, dipping them into the juice first, then pushing them together, slightly overlapping to form a secure wall so no fruit escapes. There will be enough bread left over for the top. Fill with the fruit and its juice almost right to the top. Lay the remaining bread on top of the fruit, patching up where necessary. Put the basin in a shallow dish to catch any juice that escapes, then lay a flat plate or small tray on top with a heavy weight to compact the fruit down. Leave overnight in the fridge.

5 To make the glaze, place the fruit and sugar in a pan with 4 tablespoons of water. Bring to the boil and cook for about 10 minutes over a high heat so that the fruit breaks down, releasing all the juice. Pass the fruit and juice through a sieve, use the back of a ladle to push the fruit pulp and juice through

into a pan, then stir in the cassis. The glaze should coat the back of a spoon. Cool the glaze, keep in the fridge overnight.

6 To serve, remove the weights, sliding a palette knife around the edge, pushing carefully down between bread and basin so as not to tear the bread. Put a plate on top, and then, holding the plate in place, shake firmly, lift off the basin to reveal your pudding. Spoon the cassis sauce over the top and garnish with some fresh fruit, mint leaves and rose petals.

A classic British pudding that I made in the South of France using local berries and the flavours of rose and Crème de Cassis. Just so beautiful!

Zabaglione Summer Trifles

These are easier to make than say. The zabaglione makes this trifle beautifully light and the summer berries are a delicious contrast. Making individual ones are always a nice touch for a supper party.

Ingredients

750g mixed soft summer berries

150ml Vin Santo, amaretto or marsala wine

75ml water

75g caster sugar

200g trifle sponge cake, preferably a bit stale, cut into slices

Zabaglione cream

8 large free-range egg yolks

125g caster sugar

100ml Vin Santo

300ml double cream

200g mascarpone

Large handful toasted almonds

Serves 6

What you do

1 Prepare the berries and put in a large heatproof bowl. Heat the Vin Santo with 75ml water and the sugar in a pan and boil until the sugar has dissolved, bubble to form a thick syrup (about 15 minutes). Pour it over the berries and set aside for 5 minutes.

2 Put the cake slices into 1 large trifle dish or 6 nice individual glass dishes. Using a slotted spoon, lift the fruit out of the syrup onto the sponge, spooning over some syrup to soak into the cake. Cover with cling film and chill.

3 To make the zabaglione, put the egg yolks in a large heatproof bowl with 75g of the caster sugar and the 100ml Vin Santo. Set the bowl over a pan of gently simmering water (don't let the water touch the bowl) and whisk with an electric mixer for 10-15 minutes until the mixture is very thick and pale, and leaves a ribbon-like trail when you lift the whisk; it needs to be really thick. Remove from the heat, whisk for a few more minutes until it starts to cool down, then leave to cool completely.

4 Put the remaining sugar, cream and mascarpone in a mixing bowl and whip to medium peaks. Fold into the zabaglione – it should be nice and thick.

5 Remove the trifle bowl(s) from the fridge. Crumble a handful of the toasted almonds over the fruit –keep some for finishing the trifles, then spoon the zabaglione cream on top. Chill to firm up for at least 2-3 hours then, when ready to serve, scatter with a few more toasted almonds.

Like tiramisu, this makes a great "pick me up".

Chocolate and Raspberry Tartlets

This is one of my favourite desserts – perfect, short pastry filled with smooth, rich chocolate ganache and summer ripe raspberries. It looks really elegant, cut into wedges and served with extra raspberries, along with a nice dollop of the hazelnut cream. So indulgent, but so good.

Ingredients

Pastry

250g plain flour, sifted, plus extra to roll out

75g caster sugar

125g unsalted butter, cubed

1 free-range egg yolk, beaten

A little cold water, if needed

Filling

200ml double cream

400g dark chocolate, broken into pieces

100g fresh raspberries plus 100g extra for serving

Hazelnut cream

100ml crème fraîche

2 tablespoons icing sugar, sifted

1 tablespoon Frangelico or amaretto

35g toasted hazelnuts, crushed

Serves 6-8

What you do

1 Preheat the oven to 180°C/Fan 160°C/Gas 4.

2 To make the pastry, place the flour, sugar and butter in the food processor and pulse until it resembles breadcrumbs. Add the egg yolk and process again until the pastry comes together, add a little water if needed. The dough should be soft. Alternatively make the dough by hand – put the flour in a mixing bowl, cut the butter into small pieces and rub into the flour until it all looks like buttery breadcrumbs (don't overdo it!). Stir in the sugar, make a well and add the egg yolk, mix through and begin to push into a dough, adding a teaspoon at a time of cold water, if needed. Wrap up the dough and leave to rest in the fridge for 10 minutes before rolling out.

3 Next, butter and flour a loose-bottom 22cm tart tin. Flour a clean work surface or put a piece of greaseproof paper on your work surface. Roll out the pastry dough using a floured rolling pin until it is about 3mm thick. Using the rolling pin to support the weight of the pastry, drape the pastry over the tart tin, pressing the pastry into the base and sides. The dough will be quite resilient, but work quickly. Prick the base all over, line with a sheet of baking parchment, and fill with baking beans. Chill for 20 minutes.

4 Blind bake the pastry base in the preheated oven for 25 minutes, then remove the baking beans and return the tart tin to the oven for a further 10 minutes. Take out of the oven and leave to cool in the tin.

5 Meanwhile, heat the cream in a medium-sized saucepan over a low heat. Just before it begins to boil, remove the pan from the heat and add the chocolate, leave for 5 minutes, then stir to combine.

6 Once the tart case has cooled, trim any excess pastry from around the edge, scatter the raspberries in the bottom and pour in the chocolate cream mixture. Leave to cool a little before chilling in the fridge for 30 minutes.

7 Place the crème fraîche in a small bowl, add the icing sugar, Frangelico or amaretto and all but 1 tablespoon of the hazelnuts and whisk together to thicken.

8 When you are ready to serve the tart, a quick blast with a blow torch over the surface brings the chocolate cream out to give a great gloss. Slice the tart into thick wedges using a sharp knife that has been warmed under running hot water. This will ensure a smooth finish. Place each slice on a serving plate, with a spoonful of the hazelnut crème fraîche, a few extra raspberries and a sprinkle of the remaining hazelnuts.

Roast Apricots
with Marsala Wine,
Mascarpone and
Biscotti Crumb

Ingredients

12 apricots, halved and stoned

1 vanilla pod

400ml Marsala wine

2 tablespoons honey

50g unsalted butter

To serve

4 tablespoons mascarpone

1 dessertspoon icing sugar

1 tablespoon Greek Yoghurt

2 cantuccini or 6 amaretti biscuits, crushed

Serves 4

What you do

1 Preheat the oven to to 180°C/ Fan 160°C/Gas 4.

2 Toss all the apricots into a snug ovenproof dish or roasting tin. Pour over the Marsala wine, drizzle with the honey and dot with the butter.

3 Roast for 30 minutes, or until the fruits are soft and juicy, but still retaining their shape.

4 Meanwhile, whip together the mascarpone, icing sugar and yoghurt.

5 Serve the apricots warm or chilled with their juices, with a spoonful of the mascarpone and a good sprinkle of cantuccini or amaretti biscuits.

An easy, but delicious and elegant end to a feast.

Almond Cantuccini

160g blanched almonds

300g plain flour

75g self-raising flour

125g butter, chopped

220g caster sugar

3 free range eggs, beaten lightly

5 drops almond essence

Icing sugar for dusting

Note: This recipe makes about 40 biscotti and can be made four days ahead

What you do

1 Preheat the oven to 180°C/Fan 160°C/Gas 4. Place the almonds on an oven tray and bake for about 5 minutes or until browned. Leave to cool.

2 Pulse the almonds in a food processor until finely chopped.

3 Combine the plain flour, self-raising flour and butter in a processor, then add the almonds and sugar, and combine.

4 Tip the mixture into a bowl, then stir in the eggs and almond essence. Mix it all together to form a firm dough. Flour your worksurface then knead the dough gently for 2 minutes to make a compact dough. Then divide in half, cover and refrigerate for 30 minutes.

5 Shape each half of dough into a neat 5cm x 40cm rectangle about 2cm high.

6 Slice across the dough to create slices 1cm wide. Place the slices 4cm apart on parchment-lined oven trays. Bake in the oven for about 18 minutes, or until lightly browned.

7 Transfer the cantuccini to wire racks to cool then dust with sifted icing sugar.

Peach Melba
Cheesecake

Ingredients

200g amaretti biscuits, crushed

75g unsalted butter, melted

125g caster sugar, plus extra 2 tablespoons

650g ricotta

1 tablespoon cornflour

1 teaspoon vanilla extract

4 medium free-range eggs, separated

150ml sour cream

Peach melba

4 large peaches, halved, stones removed

2 tablespoons soft brown sugar

2 tablespoons peach schnapps

200g raspberries

200ml raspberry sauce

100g redcurrants

Fresh mint sprigs

Serves 8

What you do

1 Preheat the oven to 200°C/Fan 180°C/Gas 6.

2 First, prepare the peaches – place in a roasting tin lined with parchment paper. Sprinkle over the soft brown sugar, drizzle with the peach schnapps and roast for 20-30 minutes. The peaches should be soft and there should be juices, pour the juice over the raspberries and leave to cool.

3 Next, make the cheesecake – grease and line the base of a 23cm spring form cake tin. Crush the biscuits in a food processor, then add the butter and the extra 2 tablespoons of caster sugar and mix to combine. Press into prepared pan.

4 Beat together the ricotta, 125g of the caster sugar, the cornflour, vanilla, egg yolks and sour cream.

5 In a separate clean bowl, beat the egg whites until stiff peaks form, then fold into the ricotta mixture. Pour over the base and bake for 50-60 minutes at 180°C/ Fan 160°C/ Gas 4 until pale golden and just set. Leave to cool completely and then chill for a couple of hours.

6 To assemble, put the cake onto a serving plate. Arrange the peaches on top, spoon over the raspberries, drizzle with the juices, raspberry sauce and garnish with redcurrants and mint.

Raspberry Sauce

1 150g fresh or frozen raspberries and 1 tablespoon of caster sugar boiled together for 5 minutes and passed through a sieve to form a smooth, seedless sauce.

There's always room for an indulgent dessert. Dive in!

Seasonal ingredients

June

Lamb, Wood Pigeon.

Cod, Crab, Dover Sole, Haddock, Halibut, Herring, John Dory, Lemon Sole, Lobster, Mackerel, Plaice, Salmon, Sardines, Sea Bass, Sea Tout, Grey Mullet.

Artichokes, Asparagus, Broccoli, Aubergines, Courgettes, Fennel, Mange Tout, New Potatoes, Peas, Radishes, Runner Beans, Spring Onions, Turnips, Watercress, Tomatoes, Broad Beans, Cucumbers, Kohlrabi, Salad leaves, Romaine Lettuce, Spinach, Beetroot, Green Beans.

Apricots, Blueberries, Cherries, Elderflowers, Gooseberries, Cantaloupe Melons, Raspberries, Strawberries, Blackcurrants, Plums, Redcurrants.

Special celebrations

Father's Day, Wimbledon, Royal Ascot.

July

Lamb, Rabbit, Wood Pigeon.

Plaice, Scallops, Sea Bass, Clams, Mackerel, Sardines, Cod, Crab, Dover Sole, Haddock, Halibut, Herring, John Dory, Lobster, Monkfish.

Spinach, Salad Leaves, Fennel, Radishes, Potatoes, Peas, Globe Artichokes, Cucumbers, Calabrese, Broad Beans, Heirloom Tomatoes, Garlic, Green Beans, Onions, Runner Beans.

Blueberries, Strawberries, Redcurrants, Raspberries, Rhubarb, Plums, Peaches, Nectarines, Gooseberries, Cherries, Blackcurrants, Apricots, Mulberries, Loganberries, Greengages.

Special celebrations

Royal Welsh Show.

August

Wood Pigeon, Lamb, Rabbit, Hare.

Cod, Crab, Dover Sole, Grey Mullet, Haddock, Halibut, Herring, John Dory, Lemon Sole, Lobster, Mackerel, Monkfish, Plaice, Salmon, Sardines, Scallops, Sea Bass, Squid, Turbot, Crayfish.

Artichokes, Aubergines, Beetroot, Broccoli, Broad Beans, Cabbages, Carrots, Cucumbers, Fennel, Peas, Runner Beans, Tomatoes, Courgettes, Marrow, Kohlrabi, Watercress, Chard, Sorrel, Spinach, Sweetcorn.

Raspberries, Plums, Apricots, Blackberries, Greengages, Redcurrants, Figs, Nectarines, Damsons, Loganberries, Melons.

Special celebrations

Notting Hill Carnival, Edinburgh Festival.

Summer School

There is a real energy at Llanerch Vineyard during the summer months. It is in full bloom with beautiful grounds and rolling vines creating the perfect destination for people to spend a little time relaxing. When the weather is kind, the volume of visitors almost doubles; dining al fresco is wonderful here. Taking in the views, you could almost think you are in France, sipping the local wine.

Summer is also the season for weddings and the estate offers such a magical backdrop for special celebrations. Afternoon teas are in great demand and the hotel is busy with long weekenders and those seeking a mid-week getaway. In amongst all of these happenings is the Cookery School where we encourage our guests to unwind with some focused culinary meditation.

Our classes are always set up in such a way so that when people walk in they are greeted with a display of seasonal ingredients that they will use in the dishes they prepare and cook. We include an impressive mix of vegetables, fruits, herbs and edible flowers to excite and inspire when they are with us, and when they leave they take home that ethos of seasonal importance.

Summer brings us a palette of bright and intense colours to create our dishes with, from the wonderful multi-colours of Heirloom tomatoes, the peppery tones of nasturtium flowers and the deep reds and blacks of soft summer berries, to the punchy greens found in asparagus, peas, beans and courgettes – it's our job to make the most of them.

Preparation of ingredients in class is important, learning a range of knife skills, flavour combinations and cooking methods are key to the success of each dish. The Mediterranean diet is becoming more and more popular these days and we host a range of courses that promote this style of cuisine. Many of the recipes in this book have helped to shape the courses we run during the summer months.

I love the idea of bringing people together around a table blessed with a delicious feast that is simple to share. It's reminiscent of my days working in the Mediterranean where dining was far more relaxing, eating was savoured and conversations lasted well into the night. So we try to bring some of this feeling to our classes, it's like unplugging people a little when they come to us and it's so gratifying.

At the end of a full day in the School kitchen, the air holds the aroma of good cooking scented with the accent of summer herbs and an atmosphere of achievement as everyone packs up all the dishes they have created.

We also take cooking outdoors with our Weber Grill Academy and although we do this all year round, the summer months bring us lots of people eager to make the most of the great outdoors when the sun shines. Our guests get to choose from a range of courses including "Essentials", "American", "Seafood" and the ultimate "Art of Charcoal". It's great fun and the food is excellent, everything from Italian flat bread, Beer Can Chicken and Smoked Mussels, to slow cooked smoked Brisket, Risotto and Melt in the Middle Chocolate Puddings, all cooked on the barbecue!

Our special Summer events at the School not only include our monthly Lunch Club and Saturday Morning Kitchen, but also our annual Summer Pop Up restaurant. Here we treat our guests to a rolling menu of seasonal inspired dishes and as I write this, the menu for this year has been planned and will be based on this book.

As summer eventually draws to a close, the arrival of twilight quickens and the evening air cools sharply I will be looking forward to the coming months of autumn and the promise of a great harvest with its abundance of wonderful ingredients that will form the inspiration for the next collection of recipes.

About Angela Gray

Angela opened the Cookery School at Llanerch Vineyard in 2011. The School hosts a number of special events where she cooks, chats enthusiastically and promotes the good life through cooking and eating together.

Everything that precedes her time at the School has given her the wealth of experience and knowledge needed to head such an ambitious project as a Cookery School. She worked prolifically in the food world, starting her career as a personal chef working in Europe and North America. Her clients included an esteemed list, from European aristocracy to high profile clients such as Lord Lloyd Webber. Angela took to the helm at a number of restaurants, where she developed her relaxed style of cuisine with a strong Mediterranean influence.

She returned home to Wales where her career path changed when she attended university in Cardiff and gained a BSc Honours degree in food science. Whilst studying, Angela also ran a small catering business and held a twice-monthly Cooking Club from her home. This would later form the basis of two prime time cookery series for BBC Wales, *Hot Stuff* and *More Hot Stuff*. Next came several series for radio including *My Life on a Plate* and *Packed Lunch*. She still loves to get involved in media projects, but her main focus these days is at the School and writing her cookery books.

At the close of 2016 the School was listed in the top 10 Cookery Schools in *The Independent, The Telegraph, Sunday Times* and *Evening Standard*. Most recently it was also chosen for the prestigious *National Cookery School Guide*. In her own words, that's the result of team work at its best.

Dedication

For my mother Betty – there will always be those sunny afternoons on Porthcawl beach, our simple picnics and the special quality time we shared there.

Thanks

To all the people I have worked for in the past on my travels, you gave me a free hand to be creative and develop my personal style of cooking and presenting food.

To Huw – it was great fun working with you on this project and once again the results are beautiful, the images really bring the recipes to life. Thanks to Manon for her stylish touches and my Commis Chef Ross for all your help in the studio.

To Pamela for all your support and keeping me in check, you are such a dear friend, the best!

To Sarah for managing all our social media and website, along with my thanks to all my lovely assistants.

To all the team at Graffeg.

Finally, to all my family, for the gatherings when we eat and drink together, it is always a real pleasure to feed you and to enjoy your company and simply be.

Friends of the School

AGA

Sigma 3 Kitchens

Weber Grill Academy

Ashton Fish Mongers in Cardiff Central Market

Paleo Nutrition Wales

Madhav Stores, Cardiff

Halen Mon Sea Salt

Wally's Delicatessen

Castle Dairies Welsh Salted Butter

The Softer Butter Company

Welsh Lamb and Beef

Metric and imperial equivalents

Weights	Solid	Volume	Liquid
15g	½oz	15ml	½ floz
25g	1oz	30ml	1 floz
40g	1½oz	50ml	2 floz
50g	1¾oz	100ml	3½ floz
75g	2¾oz	125ml	4 floz
100g	3½oz	150ml	5 floz (¼ pint)
125g	4½oz	200ml	7 floz
150g	5½oz	250ml	9 floz
175g	6oz	300ml	10 floz (½ pint)
200g	7oz	400ml	14 floz
250g	9oz	450ml	16 floz
300g	10½oz	500ml	18 floz
400g	14oz	600ml	1 pint (20 floz)
500g	1lb 2oz	1 litre	1¾ pints
1kg	2lb 4oz	1.2 litre	2 pints
1.5kg	3lb 5oz	1.5 litre	2¾ pints
2kg	4lb 8oz	2 litres	3½ pints
3kg	6lb 8oz	3 litres	5¼ pints

Angela's Cookbooks

Angela's cookbooks bring together a collection of recipes inspired by the seasons, her childhood, travels and career in food. They also form the basis of many of the courses run at her Cookery School in the Vale of Glamorgan at Llanerch Vineyard.

Winter Recipes

Everything naturally warms up in colour and flavour in this recipe collection. Angela uses a wide range of ingredients to invigorate the palette, from aromatic spice blends to the punchy flavours of pomegranate molasses, porcini and truffle.

Spring Recipes

Expect fresh, zesty flavours, vibrant colours and lots of inspiring ways to enhance your day-to-day cooking at home.

Summer Recipes

This book features a rich collection of recipes from Angela's travels and her time spent working in the South of France. Barbecuing, dining al fresco, entertaining friends, it's all here.

Autumn Recipes

Colours and flavours become richer and deeper in this book and recipes embrace the wonderful harvest of seasonal ingredients. Angela shares easy ways to entertain so you can be the host with the most.

Festive Recipes

The highlight of the Cookery School Calendar is the "Festive Kitchen" event, where Angela demonstrates a range of inspirational recipes that are all show stoppers, guaranteed to "wow" friends and family throughout the Christmas and New Year celebrations. This is her very special collection of those recipes.

'I love the way life naturally slows down a little in the kitchen during the Summer months, from preparing and cooking simple dishes, to longer, relaxed evenings around the dining table with friends'